Designed by Flowerpot Press
www.FlowerpotPress.com
CHC-0909-0592
ISBN: 978-1-4867-2565-6
Made in China/Fabriqué en Chine

HOW DOES WATER MOVE AROUND?

A BOOK ABOUT THE WATER CYCLE

written by maddine j. hayes

illustrated by srimalie bassani

LAKE

OCEAN

We drink it, swim in it, clean ourselves with it, and play in it—water is essential for life. Plants, animals, and humans all need water to survive. The good news? Water is all around us and constantly cycling so that we never run out. Water has been on our planet since the beginning of time. The way water cycles and replenishes is necessary and also interesting, so let's learn some more!

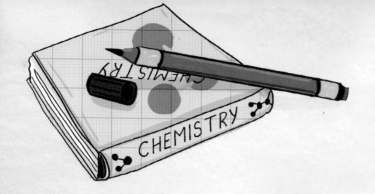

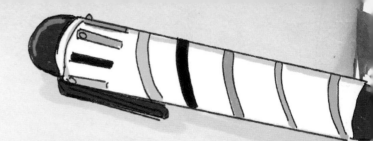

How does water move through the air?
Can it fly around using superpowers?

Water actually can kind of fly because it floats around in the air. It also keeps us alive, so that seems pretty super to me!

Super water!

CHEMISTRY

the water cycle

WATER MOLECULE

H_2O

Water is also known as H_2O because it is made up of one part oxygen (O) and two parts hydrogen (H). Hydrogen and oxygen are the elements that bind together to make up a single molecule of water. Molecules are really tiny though, so when you see running water in a sink or a river, you're actually seeing lots and lots of water molecules all moving around each other.

water vapor   liquid water   solid water

Water can come in all shapes and sizes. It can be a solid (like ice), a liquid (like drinking water), or a gas (we call this water vapor).

Water vapor is constantly moving through the air all around us; we just can't see it because it is super tiny. The molecules in water vapor are spread farther apart from each other than when water is in solid or liquid form.

Have you ever noticed how it feels extra humid and sticky outside right before it rains? This is because there is a larger than normal amount of water in the air around you and your skin can feel it even when you can't see it.

Lemonade is my favorite liquid!

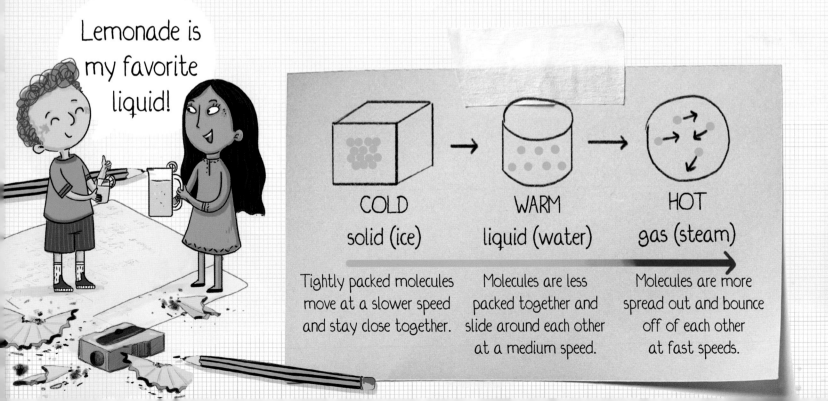

COLD	WARM	HOT
solid (ice)	liquid (water)	gas (steam)
Tightly packed molecules move at a slower speed and stay close together.	Molecules are less packed together and slide around each other at a medium speed.	Molecules are more spread out and bounce off of each other at fast speeds.

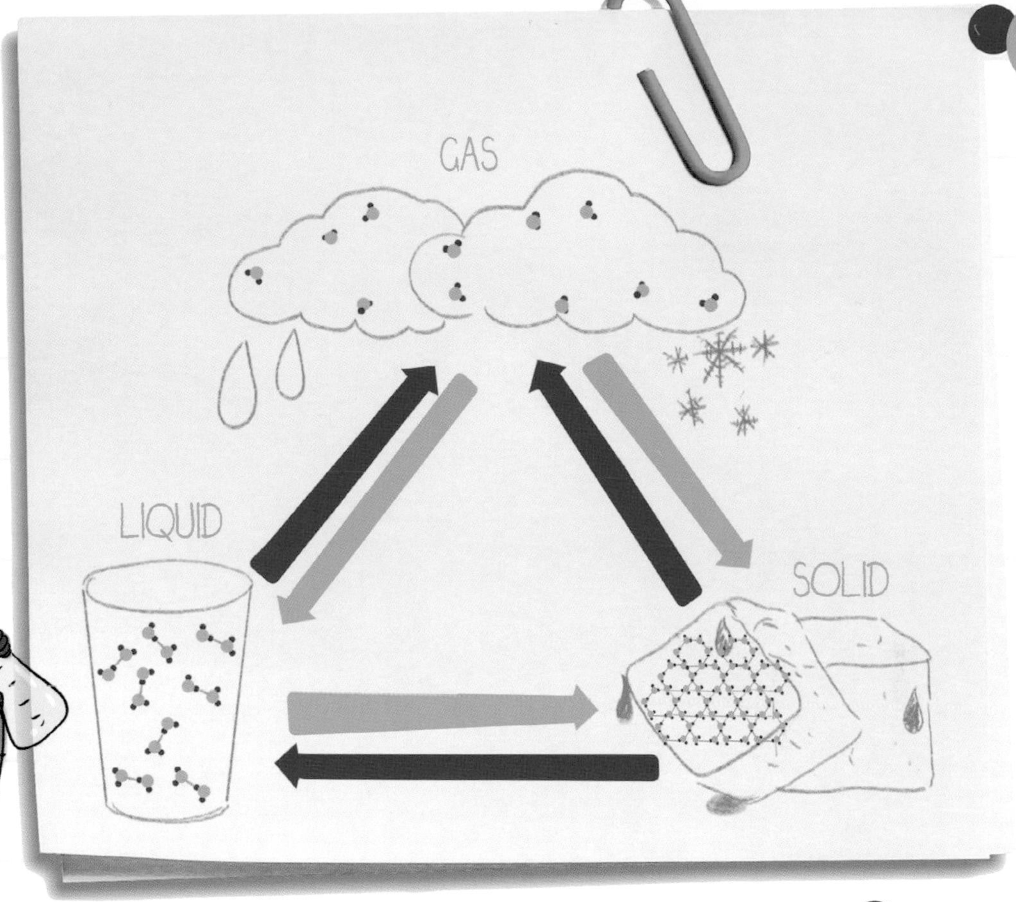

GAS

LIQUID

SOLID

Have you ever seen mist or fog in the early morning? That's water too! Rain is liquid water moving through the air and snow is solid water moving through the air. There is water all around us whether we realize it or not!

How does water move around on the ground?
Does it hitch a ride on the back of bugs?

We have enough water for a month!

Well not on the back of bugs necessarily, but animals do help move water around on Earth—that includes you! We already talked about how water can move in the air, but how does it move around on the ground? There are all sorts of ways!

Hey buddy! I'm drinking here!

People and animals consume water by drinking it and then they move it around throughout their day when they sweat or go to the bathroom or sneeze. When they do this, they release water into the world in a different spot than they consumed it. You move water around without even realizing you're doing it!

We also physically make water move through pipes to come out of faucets, sinks, showers, and toilets.

When you start looking, you will see water moving all around us constantly, which is great, because without a shower we would all stink!

Where does all this water come from?

rain

UNDERGROUND WATER

Water also moves around on Earth without the help of animals and humans. When water falls to Earth's surface, it can get absorbed into the ground and move through the soil. This is how plants and trees get their water. They absorb it through their roots and then it moves through the plant to get to where it's needed most.

Look at all that water!

Ohhh, so that's where it's collected!

Water also flows naturally over land and gathers in puddles, rivers, lakes, and oceans. Oceans are the biggest source of water movement on Earth's surface. About 97% of the water on our planet is collected in the oceans, and oceans cover about 71% of Earth's surface—that's a lot of water!

RIVERS

LAKES

PONDS

OCEANS AND SEAS

Come play with us!

How does water move around in the sky? Does it jump from cloud to cloud?

It doesn't jump from cloud to cloud—it MAKES the clouds! When water gets into the air, water vapor will naturally move upwards with the air (remember water vapor is in the air all around us, we just can't see it). When water vapor gets high enough in the atmosphere, it starts to cool down. When it cools down, the water becomes liquid or ice and clusters together with other water molecules. This is how clouds are formed.

A cloud is a group of tiny water droplets, snowflakes, or small ice crystals that we can see in the air!

cloud

heat from the sun

water vapor begins to cool

rising warm air

water vapor

liquid water

ground

A cloud is a big grouping of water molecules that are transforming from a vapor back into liquid and solid water. They don't just appear out of nowhere. They are formed by the water molecules already in the air. The temperature, wind, and atmospheric conditions determine what shape the cloud is, where it is located, and where it moves. Clouds and water vapor can get shifted by the wind and transfer water all around our atmosphere. When a cloud gets big and heavy enough, the water molecules fall back down to the ground.

TYPES OF CLOUDS

HIGH CLOUDS

cirrus

cirrocumulus

cirrostratus

MID-LEVEL CLOUDS

altostratus

altocumulus

cumulonimbus

LOW CLOUDS

stratocumulus

cumulus

stratus

Why do clouds start to rain?
Is it because giants are crying in the sky?

FUN FACT

In certain dry climates,
rain can evaporate before it even
hits the ground, so it can rain
but not be wet. This type of
rain is called virga.

No way, rain isn't a sad thing—it's a happy thing! We need rain to get water returning to Earth's surface where we can use it! But how does the rain get there? We have talked a lot about water moving around in the sky and on the ground and we know that it can exist in the air around us, but let's focus a little bit more on how it moves from the air to the ground. When water vapor cools and turns into a liquid or ice, that is a process known as condensation. Condensation is what happens when a gas turns into a liquid. This is why when water vapor rises into the air and cools down it becomes a cloud.

Look what happened to my glass!

FUN FACT
Condensation is why water droplets form on the outside of your water glass on a hot day. The water vapor in the air cools when it bumps into the cold glass and becomes a liquid, which then slides down your glass in droplets.

cold water →

condensation →

water (liquid) →

warm, moist air

When enough water cools down and the clouds become too heavy, water falls to the ground as rain, snow, or hail, depending on how cold it is in the air. This is called precipitation. Precipitation is the step between water being in a cloud and water landing on the ground. It is how the water gets to Earth's surface. Depending on the temperature of the air, the water droplets can come down as liquid water in the form of rain, or if it is really cold, the water droplets transform on their way to the ground into a solid in the form of snow or hail.

TYPES OF PRECIPITATION

RAIN forms when the water droplets in clouds get too heavy and begin to fall to the ground.

HAIL forms when water droplets freeze and strong winds carry them higher into a cloud before falling back down to the ground.

SNOW forms when the temperature of the air is below freezing, causing the falling water droplets to form into snow.

How does liquid water turn into a vapor? Do fairies cast a spell on it to make it float?

That can't be right! This is the part of the water cycle in which water goes from the ground to the sky, but how did it get up there in the first place? The missing piece of the puzzle is a process known as evaporation. Evaporation is when a liquid turns into a vapor (it is the opposite of condensation).

The sun is the secret agent in charge of getting water back into the sky, so it can continue to cycle. We rely on the sun to heat up water molecules on Earth's surface enough to transform them back into vapor form, where they will naturally rise into the atmosphere. This happens because hot air rises. Without the sun, evaporation wouldn't be possible. Water can evaporate from anywhere though, most commonly from the oceans, because that is where most of our water is stored.

One specific example of evaporation is when plants release water into the atmosphere around them through tiny holes in their leaves. This is a very helpful process in the water cycle and it is called transpiration. Transpiration is what happens when water evaporates directly from plants into the atmosphere.

See it for yourself! Place a full cup of water in the sun. Use a marker to make a line at the top of the water level. Each hour, mark the water level and begin to look for changes. As the sun heats the water, it should begin to evaporate.

1 hour
2 hours
3 hours

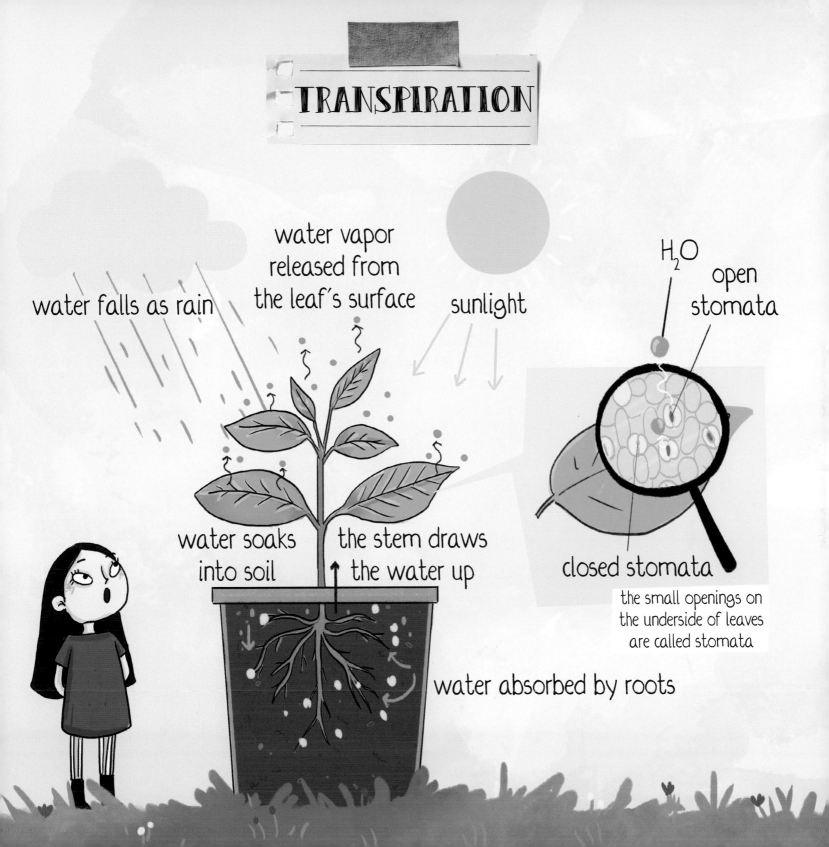

How do we get more water? Does it get shipped in from outer space?

Trick question! We don't get more water. We reuse the water we've been using since the beginning of time! The water we use today is the same water we have had on our planet for millions and millions of years, and in that time it's been all over the world in different forms. Maybe you've gotten the picture by now, but water is constantly cycling all around us.

If you could follow one water molecule with a tiny tracker, you would see it move in a giant circle. A drop of water could start by evaporating right out of your hand and into the air, where it would travel up, up, up into the sky. Then that same water could condense back into a droplet and become a small part of a big cloud with a bunch of its friends. The water droplet could then precipitate and fall back to the ground. It could land in someone else's hand, or in the ocean, or maybe it'll water a plant so it can grow big and strong. The important thing is that it keeps cycling over and over again.

The water we drink today could have been used in a dinosaur's bath!

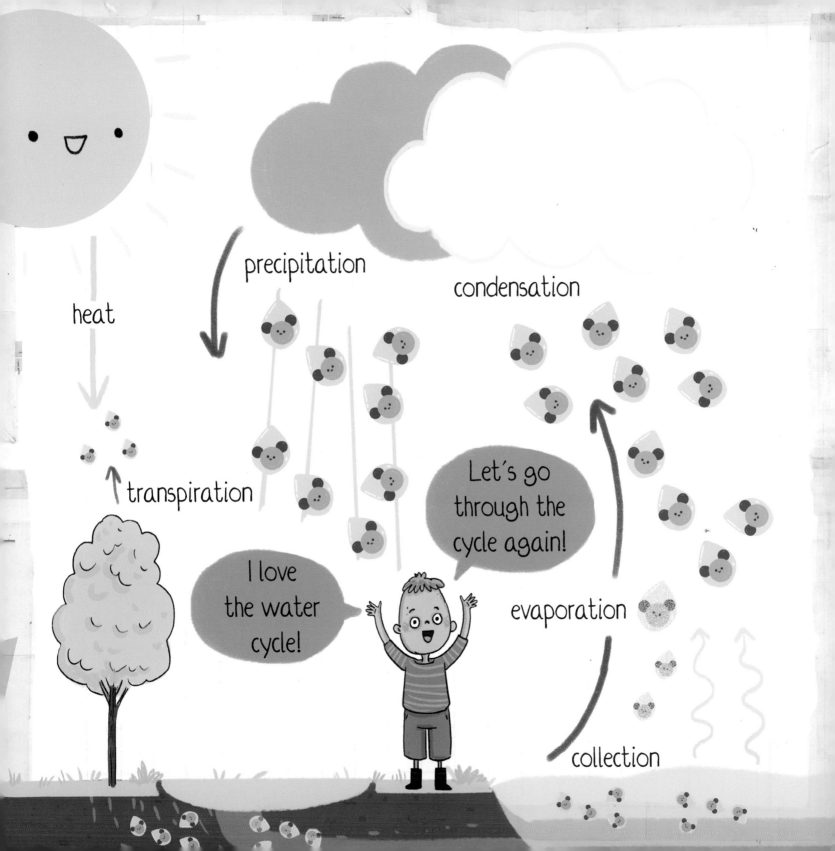

As you have learned, we need water for survival. When the water cycle gets disrupted or when we don't conserve water as much as possible, we run the risk of using water faster than it can get replenished naturally. This causes harsh weather called droughts, where rain stops falling for long periods of time. Droughts make the land dry up and can kill plants that we rely on for food and energy. When this happens in extremes, it can also cause more natural disasters, such as forest fires. While this is scary, there are things we can do to help fight it and support the water cycle. We can conserve water whenever possible. Conserving water simply means being careful how we use it and not wasting it.

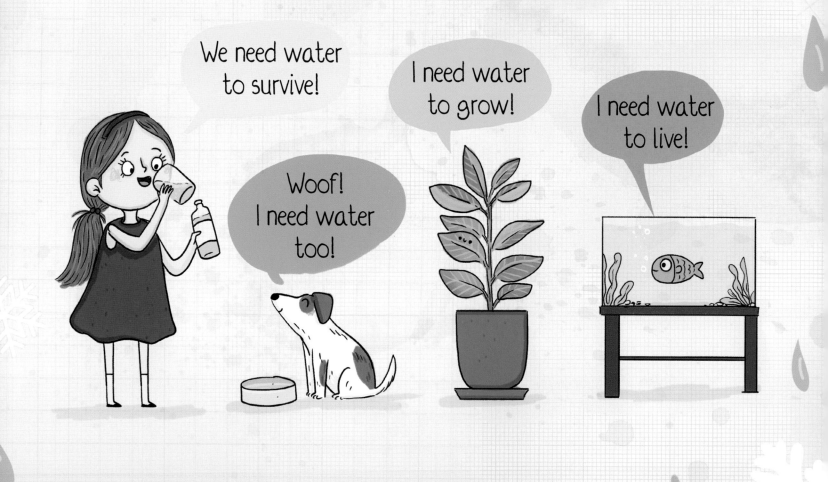

HOW TO CONSERVE WATER

There are small steps you can take at home to make sure you're helping to conserve water.

You can collect rain and reuse it in your garden!

Take shorter showers when you can!

Also check to make sure your faucets aren't leaking!

Turn the tap off when brushing your teeth or washing your hands!

Try to only put full loads in the washing machine!

THE WATER CYCLE

1 CONDENSATION
This is the part of the water cycle in which water vapor rises into the air and where it turns into water droplets and forms clouds. The water goes from a gas to a liquid.

2 PRECIPITATION
Once clouds become too heavy, the water droplets making up the cloud fall back down to the ground in the form of snow, rain, hail, or sleet. The water either stays liquid or turns into a solid.

3 TRANSPIRATION
This is what happens when plants release water from their leaves into the air. The water goes from a liquid to a gas.

4 EVAPORATION
When the sun heats up the earth, it causes water, mainly from lakes, oceans, and rivers, to evaporate into the air. The water goes from a liquid to a gas.

5 DEPOSITION
This happens when water in the air goes directly from being a gas to being a solid, for example when you see frost on the ground. The water goes from a gas to a solid.

6 SUBLIMATION
This is what happens when water goes from being a cold solid to a gas. This can happen in cold temperatures and high elevations, like at the top of a mountain. The water goes from a solid to a gas.

7 COLLECTION
When water falls to the earth, it collects in lakes, rivers, and oceans where it can begin the cycle again.

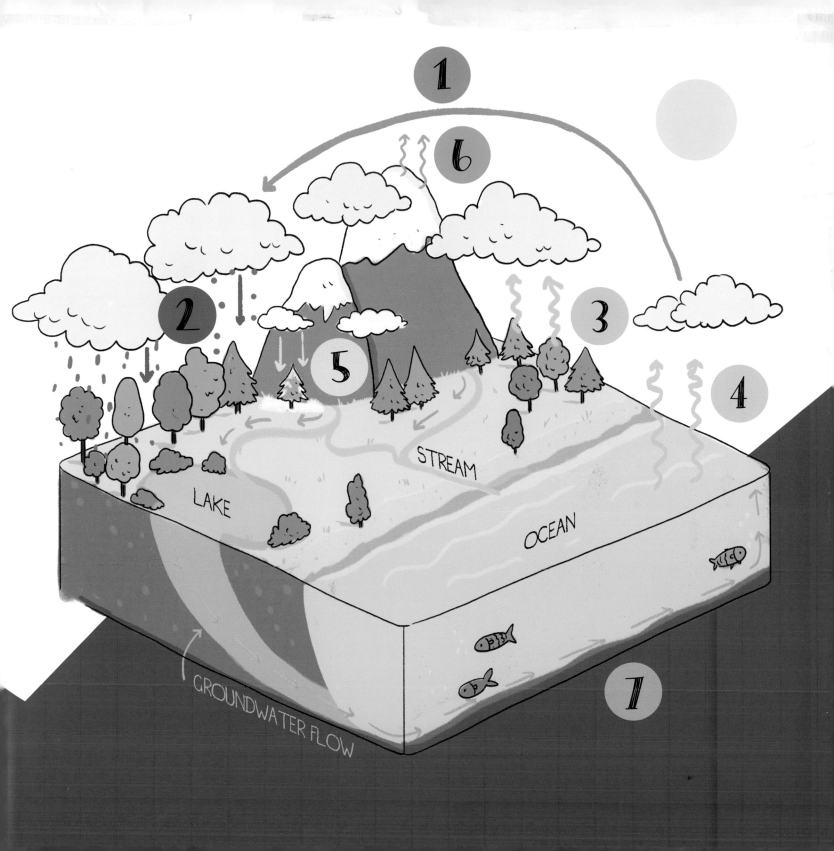

WATER CYCLE IN A BAG

Make your very own miniature water cycle using just a few things you have around your home.

MATERIALS:

- Resealable plastic bag
- Permanent marker
- Water
- Food coloring
- Tape

INSTRUCTIONS:

1 Use your marker to draw some clouds and a sun on the outside of your resealable plastic bag. The clouds and sun should be toward the top of your bag.

2 Add 2 cups (480 milliliters) of water and 2 drops of food coloring into your bag and seal so that no water can escape.

3 Tape your water bag to a window that gets plenty of sunlight. Make sure the sealable part of your bag is at the top.

4 Check back on your bag every couple of hours and observe how the water has moved around inside the bag. You should slowly see the water in your bag move through the water cycle!

WHAT YOU WILL SEE:

- When there is less water in the bottom of the bag, that means some of it has evaporated.
- When water collects at the top of the bag where the clouds are drawn, that is an example of condensation.
- When the condensation becomes too much and the water falls down the side of the bag back to the bottom, this is an example of precipitation.

All of this is made possible by the heat from the sun. We need the sun to make the water cycle possible!

GLOSSARY

Atmosphere – the layer of gases above a planet

Cloud – a collection of water droplets in the sky

Condensation – when water molecules cool down enough to change from a gas to a liquid

Conservation – preserving or protecting something

Deposition – when water molecules change from a gas to a solid

Drought – a period of time without precipitation

Evaporation – when water molecules heat up enough to change from a liquid to a gas

Freezing – when water molecules cool down enough to change from a liquid to a solid

Gas – a state of matter that can change shape and volume

Hydrogen – a gaseous element, the most abundant in the world; makes water when two hydrogen atoms are combined with one oxygen atom

Liquid – a state of matter that can change shape but not volume

Melting – when molecules heat up enough to change from a solid to a liquid

Oxygen – a gaseous element, required to sustain life; makes water when combined with two hydrogen atoms

Precipitation – when water, in the form of rain, sleet, snow, or hail, falls from clouds

Solid – a state of matter that cannot change shape or volume

Stomata – collection of pores on a plant through which water vapor can escape

Sublimation – when water molecules change from a solid to a gas

Transpiration – when water vapor escapes through the stomata of a plant

Water cycle – the continuous flow of water throughout Earth, as a solid, liquid, and gas

Water molecule – substance made up of two hydrogen atoms and one oxygen atom

Water vapor – the gaseous form of water